Heart
MATTERS

Juanita Bynum

Charisma
HOUSE
A STRANG COMPANY

Most STRANG COMMUNICATIONS/CHARISMA HOUSE/SILOAM/FRONTLINE/REALMS products are available at special quantity discounts for bulk purchase for sales promotions, premiums, fund-raising, and educational needs. For details, write Strang Communications/Charisma House/Siloam/FrontLine/Realms, 600 Rinehart Road, Lake Mary, Florida 32746, or telephone (407) 333-0600.

HEART MATTERS by Juanita Bynum
Published by Charisma House
A Strang Company
600 Rinehart Road
Lake Mary, Florida 32746
www.charismahouse.com

Unless otherwise noted, all Scripture quotations are from the Amplified Bible. Old Testament copyright © 1965, 1987 by the Zondervan Corporation. The Amplified New Testament copyright © 1954, 1958, 1987 by the Lockman Foundation. Used by permission.

Scripture quotations marked KJV are from the King James Version of the Bible.

Cover design by Judith McKittrick
Interior design by Terry Clifton

Library of Congress Cataloging-in-Publication Data

Bynum, Juanita.
  Heart matters / Juanita Bynum.
    p. cm.
  ISBN 978-1-59979-058-9 (casebound)
  1. Spirituality. 2. Heart--Religious aspects--Christianity. I. Title.
  BV4501.3.B97 2006
  248.4--dc22

                              2006023585

Adapted from *Matters of the Heart* by Juanita Bynum, published by Charisma House, copyright © 2002, ISBN 0-88419-832-4.

07 08 09 10 11 — 987654321
Printed in the United States of America

CONTENTS

The Heart

CHAPTER I

of the Matter

What is the condition of your heart toward God and toward His people?

WOULD YOU LIKE TO EXPERIENCE THE FULLNESS OF GOD'S LOVE? In this little book I want to get to the heart of the matter—the condition of your heart. You will experience the fullness of God's love when you have exchanged your "old heart," full of self and things that keep God's love from flowing into your heart and life—for a "new heart." This exchange will be a heart transplant that brings total spiritual transformation.

So stop trying to fix the old—let God give you something new. I want to show you the steps to your own heart transformation by letting you see how God showed me my own need for a new heart.

It happened unexpectedly. I knew that I was saved—born and raised in the church, for that matter. I had grown up in the ministry and then moved on into my own full-time ministry, so I was used to the routine. Certain things were just part of my personality...had been for many years. I didn't realize it at that moment, but it was time for a change.

Right before we held the Chicago Summit in May of 2000, we had held a summit in Pensacola, Florida—which did not turn out the way that I thought it should have. We had rented a ten-thousand-seat auditorium, and only about six to seven thousand attendees showed up. But it wasn't just the attendance; across the board the conference did not turn out the way that I had hoped. Immediately after that conference, I started carrying a burden—Pensacola had been unsuccessful.

As the date approached for the Chicago Summit, the Lord began to get my attention. We were planning to have the event in a beautiful church that seated forty-five hundred people. It was going to be impressive. You see, I was determined, because of what had "happened" in Pensacola, that I was going to make the Chicago Summit go over the top—everything was going to be just right.

Then I was hit with the unexpected. One day, just as I pulled up to my garage, the phone rang. My assistant, Tonya, explained that we were not going to be able to use the "beautiful" facility and that we had to switch to another facility. It was not as big and was more difficult for the people to get to. When she was finished, I hung up and began to weep.

As the tears rolled down my face, God said, "You are thinking like man. You are always concerned about the

The most important thing is to have the new heart and to know that you have it!

outward appearance. You are always trying to make that outward image look acceptable." He continued, "Jesus made Himself of no reputation, yet it is your reputation that has become most important to you. You are thinking about all that you are doing, the major platforms where you are able to speak, and all the exposure that you are getting. But what is the condition of your heart toward Me and toward My people?"

I sat there in my driveway, confused, and said to the Lord, "My heart? You know that everything I am doing, I am doing to please You."

He responded, "You are not doing what you can to please Me. You are doing what you can to please people. You are doing what you can to be accepted by people."

Then He began to show me how my burden for the Pensacola Summit was not really about whether the people had or had not been blessed. They *were* blessed. But the truth was that I had left that conference wondering, *What are people going to say because the auditorium was not filled? What are people going to say because this or that thing was not right? What are people going to say because the flyers looked homemade?*

God said, "Let Me show you some little things." He started surfacing things about my personality, things I had reasoned were "just me"—but, really, they were errors in my heart. He said, "The sad thing is, you are so far away from Me. You are nowhere near Me though you think that you are."

He took me to Ephesians 2:8, which says that we are not saved "by works." Then He continued, "You need to accept the fact that I am making you the 'righteousness of God.' You have been working under the assumption that all of your works have impressed Me, and I am not impressed by any of it."

Finally He said, "The reason that I am not impressed is because you are so far away from the goal that I have set for you. You are racing, trying to 'make it happen' on a big scale in auditoriums and all of that. But what about the little, everyday people whom I put on your heart to be a blessing to? You have ignored that because you think nobody can see it."

God dealt with me as I sat there in my driveway. He said, "I want to give you a new heart."

"A new heart?" I asked. "But I already feel like I am saved."

Many of God's people think the way I thought. We assume that we operate from our personalities, that we have a certain style—a *modus operandi*—when, really, it is a much deeper matter. In actuality, our preconceived thought patterns move us far away from God's character and from what He expects from us as His children.

So many of us want to concentrate our efforts on our "overt" walk with the Lord, one where we are more interested in what others think than we are with what

A person who maintains the reins of his heart and controls the patterns of his mind impresses God.

God thinks about us. We constantly try to "fix up" what people see about us.

A Real Conversion? A True Salvation?

I was not expecting to receive a "new heart" message. I felt that I had given my heart to God when I was converted, but somewhere along the way it had gone into a dormant state. I knew that I had accepted Christ as my personal Savior. My spirit man, or my heart, was converted, and I began to get into the Word. You see, I wanted to transform my mind so that my life could begin to experience what had happened in my heart. Then somewhere along the line, I started reading the Word of God to prepare me to preach the gospel—not to convert my own mind.

When I began doing this, even though I was preaching a powerful gospel, I was having difficulties and struggles in my personal life, constantly warring against the flesh. My mind warred against my heart, and my heart warred against my mind. I could never seem to bring my thoughts and emotions under subjection to my converted heart.

My ministry became my career, and even though I knew that I had been called to preach, I believe it was God's compassion for His people that kept me there. Hear me. When God's people cried out in the Old Testament, He would supply what they needed because He had heard their cry. His heart is tender toward His people. So when I said to Him that I was willing to "go," and there was a cry from His people, He anointed me and used me in His work.

Yet God loved me so much that He said, "While you are preaching to others, I do not want to forget about you."

THE TRUE HEART REVEALED

The Lord took me to Jeremiah 17:9–10, where He said:

> The heart is deceitful above all things, and it is exceedingly perverse and corrupt and severely, mortally sick! Who can know it [perceive, understand, be acquainted with his own heart and mind]? I the Lord search the mind, I try the heart, even to give to every man according to his ways, according to the fruit of his doings.

God had tried my heart, and I had failed the test. As a result, in all the good that I was doing, my heart still wore the core of wickedness.

If we are not careful, we can be doing a religious work and still be backslidden in our hearts. We can do this without realizing it, either because our works are so wonderful or because the responses our works are getting are so wonderful. We may even feel God's anointing and presence upon our works, which can, in itself, become a deception. How? Our works can be so "good" that we never stop to recheck our heart to see if it is found in right standing with God.

> When we pursue the image of perfection, we cannot understand the heart of God.

So how can this "old heart," which was "born in sin" and "shaped in iniquity," love God? Real love cannot come out of this heart. Only a *phileo* kind of love (which means the natural human affection, with its strong feeling, or sentiment) can come from a wicked heart. *Agape* love (unconditional and eternal) is never found in our "old hearts." The only way that you can truly love God is to love Him with the same love that He has given to you.

Loving God brings about a commitment to Him. When you love somebody, you are committed to him in every way. There is nothing that you will not do for someone you love. You would be willing to lay down your life for your loved one. So when you say, "I love You, Lord," but still walk in your own ways, then you do not really love the Lord. You are still going about in your "religious affairs," and you do not have a real relationship with Him, which will bring about a change of character and a change in the way you walk. A real relationship with Him enables you to walk in His commandments.

If you do not have a real relationship with Him, then you merely "appreciate" Him for the life and breath that He has given you. You are grateful that He makes a way for you out of no way and for all the things He permits you to have. But you are still operating from a materialistic standpoint—and that is not real love. It cannot become real until you become committed and submitted to His ways.

My *Heart Matters*

What's Wrong

CHAPTER 2

With the
Old Heart?

The heart is deceitful.

WHAT ABOUT OUR OLD HEART? IS IT SIM-
PLY A "POOR, LITTLE, CONFUSED, MESSED-UP
HEART"? Is it really possible that your heart is the thing
preventing you from experiencing the intimacy and close-
ness to God that you crave...that you are longing for?

You can begin to understand the condition of your
old heart by taking a closer look at Jeremiah 17:9:

> The heart is deceitful above all things, and it is exceed-
> ingly perverse and corrupt and severely, mortally sick!
> Who can know it [perceive, understand, be acquainted
> with his own heart and mind]?

In this verse the word *deceitful* means "to mislead by a
false appearance or statement; to trick." We must recognize, first and foremost, that God called the old heart "deceitful above all things." It does not matter how much you
try...how many Bible studies you attend...or what Bible
classes you take. I do not care how many times you say, "If I
can just go to church and sing in the choir, everything will
be all right."

No! Remember that this wicked heart misleads not only other people, but it also misleads *you*. This heart gives a false appearance, not just to people, but also to *you*. It makes you think, *Because I look right, I am right*.

But there is another definition for the word *deceitful* that startled me—it also means "to be unfaithful." The saddest fact about this heart—and again, shockingly so—is

> The heart determines whether or not you enter the kingdom of God.

that it is unfaithful. It can never be dedicated to God. It can never keep a commitment. Maybe this is the reason why people constantly move in and out of relationships, or why the divorce rate is so high. Perhaps it is the reason why so many children are living in orphanages, or why prostitution is rampant. Maybe it is even why there is such a lack of integrity in the body of Christ.

If we do not ask for and receive a new heart, deception spreads like a virus. What are the telltale signs of a diseased heart? The parable Jesus tells in Matthew 13 about the sower of seed will show us some of the symptoms of a diseased heart.

SOIL ALONG THE ROADSIDE

Listen to the [meaning of the] parable of the sower: While anyone is hearing the Word of the kingdom and does not grasp and comprehend it, the evil one comes and snatches away what was sown in his heart. This is what was sown along the roadside.

—MATTHEW 13:18–19

How is the "evil one" able to snatch a Word that has been sown in someone's heart? He is familiar with the grounds. He (Satan) already knows that the Word is trying to penetrate that heart; he knows that the base character of that heart does not have what it takes to absorb and to hold that Word. The enemy knows already that the Word is sitting in a heart that has been consumed by the spirit of perverseness.

Have you ever known somebody who heard the Word of the Lord and then tried to change its meaning in order to justify his sin? This is what happens when the old heart is in operation. Satan, already familiar with the ground within that heart because he lives and rules there, projects himself there because he does not have a home. He takes control of that ground because the heart is filled with all of the enemy's works. That heart is filled with his ungodly character, and he will not allow anything that is righteous and holy to remain there.

At the point when the Word of the Lord tries to penetrate into that heart, holy things are illegally trespassing on the enemy's ground. He has taken possession of that old heart. Satan has "grounds" to operate anywhere that he gains a legal precedent. The earth realm is "legal" ground for Satan. This is why believers must walk in the Spirit.

God warns that if you do not walk in the Spirit (and the way to walk in the Spirit is to receive the "new heart" of the Spirit), then Satan can take anything righteous that hits those grounds. He has a legal right to cancel it! You have given the right to him. Your heart is diseased and has become foreign ground, exhibiting the symptoms of sin disease.

> *This deceitful heart does not have what it takes to be faithful to anything—God or man.*

ROCKY SOIL

As for what was sown on thin (rocky) soil, this is he who hears the Word and at once welcomes and accepts it with joy.

—MATTHEW 13:20

Are you seeing the revelation—*emotionalism*? Many people hear the Word and "accept it with joy." You can see it every Sunday in the church. People hollering back at the preacher, shouting, "Amen, preach it!" all over the church. Yet the Bible says:

> …it has no real root in him, but is temporary (inconstant, lasts but a little while); and when affliction or trouble or persecution comes on account of the Word, at once he is caused to stumble [he is repelled and begins to distrust and desert Him Whom he ought to trust and obey] and he falls away.
>
> —MATTHEW 13:21

God is describing people who hear the Word, but there is no real heart penetration. There is no depth to where His Word can be planted. It floats around in the "emotional" realm, and when something else "exciting" charges these emotions in a different way and direction, the first Word is canceled out. The emotions, which are fleshly, take precedence at that moment over the Word of God. The Word does not reside in this heart, and it cannot find a resting place.

THORNY SOIL

As for what was sown among thorns, this is he who hears the Word, but the cares of the world and the pleasure and delight and glamour and deceitfulness of riches choke and suffocate the Word, and it yields no fruit.

—MATTHEW 13:22

The Word of the Lord cannot be implanted into the old heart. In order for the Word of the Lord to penetrate and take root in our lives, we must have a new heart. We must unseat Satan from his throne in our lives. James 1:21 tells us how to do that:

So get rid of all uncleanness and the rampant outgrowth of wickedness, and in a humble (gentle, modest) spirit receive and welcome the Word which implanted and rooted [in your hearts] contains the power to save your souls.

The Bible tells us that once we have that new heart, we are to:

…be doers of the Word [obey the message], and not merely listeners to it, betraying yourselves [into deception by reasoning contrary to the Truth].

—JAMES 1:22

People who do not have the "new heart" hear the truth and then start "betraying" themselves through deceit (reasoning). They rationalize that truth and come up with every reason why "this is not what the Bible means." Their hearts are so filled with the world and the things of the world that they are deceived into thinking they have all they need.

Don't allow the "world and the pleasure and delight and glamour and deceitfulness of riches" to "choke and suffocate the Word" when God attempts to penetrate your heart with it. Don't let these "good" things choke the Word out of your heart! That is perversion.

For if anyone only listens to the Word without obeying it and being a doer of it, he is like a man who looks carefully at his [own] natural face in a mirror; for he thoughtfully observes himself, and then goes off and promptly forgets what he was like.

—JAMES 1:23–24

A pattern repeats throughout the Bible—we need a new heart. Why? Let us look at one example of a "good heart" to see what God desires.

The new heart causes us to see the things of God.

GOOD SOIL

As for what was sown on good soil, this is he who hears the Word and grasps and comprehends it; he indeed bears fruit and yields in one case a hundred times as much as was sown, in another sixty times as much, and in another thirty.

—MATTHEW 13:23

The person represented in this parable about the good soil has a converted heart. This person, who has received a new heart, has an "active" Word on the inside. God's spoken Word comes alive and produces good fruit. This Word has the power to save and the power to keep. How do I know it is operative? Hebrews 4:12 says:

> For the Word that God speaks is alive and full of power [making it active, operative, energizing, and effective]; it is sharper than any two-edged sword, penetrating to the dividing line of the breath of life (soul) and [the immortal] spirit, and of joints and marrow [of the deepest parts of our nature], exposing and sifting and analyzing and judging the very thoughts and purposes of the heart.

The penetrating Word is filled with power! It energizes your spirit, heart, and soul as it accomplishes God's will. This Word can never be stagnated. It goes down into the intricate parts of the inner man and "dissects" everything it finds there. When the enemy comes in "like a flood," that Word knows how to swim. When the fire rages, that Word knows how to hold its breath. When the wind starts blowing, that Word is anchored. When the sun starts to blaze, that Word knows how to get in the shade—regardless of what life's temperature may be.

When the Word takes up residence in this heart, it operates with divine power and produces more fruit. This heart embraces the Word it has received and produces more than it has been given. The Word that goes into a "new heart" is active. It "identifies" with the divine nature of God and multiplies.

My *Heart Matters*

How Do You
Need a

Chapter 3

Know You
New Heart?

1

You have become insensitive to the fact that you are living a reckless life before God.

$\mathcal{H}$OW DO YOU KNOW WHEN YOU NEED A NEW HEART? How do you know the difference between making a mistake and falling away from your first love? Revelation 2:4–5 (KJV) warns:

> Nevertheless I have somewhat against thee, because thou hast left thy first love. Remember therefore from whence thou art fallen, and repent, and do the first works; or else I will come unto thee quickly, and will remove thy candlestick out of his place, except thou repent.

A STEP-BY-STEP PROCESS

Ephesians 4 gives us a step-by-step process to teach us to recognize when we have fallen away from our first love and need a new heart.

> So this I say and solemnly testify [in the name of] the Lord [as in His presence], that you must no longer live as the heathen (the Gentiles) do in their perverseness [in the folly, vanity, and emptiness of their souls and the futility] of their minds.

—EPHESIANS 4:17

1. A "futile" mind is incapable of producing any result.

Remember that a "futile" mind is incapable of producing any result; it is ineffective, useless, and unsuccessful. The thought patterns of this mind do not yield anything that is fruitful or beneficial. This first step is when we look at things our own way and pervert the Word of God.

2. Our moral understanding is darkened.

"Their moral understanding is darkened and their reasoning is beclouded" (v. 18). This is the second step. When you start doing ungodly things and yet try to justify why you are doing it, your moral understanding is darkened, and your reasoning is beclouded.

3. We explain away our actions according to worldly knowledge and carnal information.

"[They are] alienated (estranged, self-banished) from the life of God [with no share in it: this is] because of the ignorance (the want of knowledge and perception)" (v. 18). We are living in a brain world. This world moves according to knowledge, not according to the new heart.

It is propelled by the mind and the lust for knowledge, which bring personal power. Everybody is in a sweat to gain more information and knowledge. Yet they are still

> *Your heart can be deceived without your knowing it, because you live for God from the "religious factor."*

ignorant about God and His ways; they are like the people described in 2 Timothy 3:7, who "are never able to arrive at a recognition and knowledge of the Truth."

As a result, we try to cover our actions by "explaining them away" according to worldly knowledge and carnal information. Gaining this knowledge and information can, once again, deceive the old heart into thinking, *I am filled with great knowledge; therefore, I have an understanding of*

God. Not so. You may read the Bible and comprehend it according to the English language, but the only way that you can understand it according to the Spirit is by virtue of the new heart.

4. We persistently do things our own way.

Ephesians 4:18 continues, "(...the willful blindness) that is deep-seated in them, due to their hardness of heart [to the insensitiveness of their moral nature]." This is step four—persistently doing things our way. We have become willfully blinded, not incapable of seeing. We have chosen it. That is why this verse says the blindness is "deep-seated." We have been doing something a certain way for years and years, until we finally believe that we are walking in God's ways when in fact we are in error. Our hearts have become hardened and insensitive to what is right before God:

> In their spiritual apathy they have become callous and past feeling and reckless and have abandoned themselves [a prey] to unbridled sensuality, eager and greedy to indulge in every form of impurity [that their depraved

desires may suggest and demand]. But you did not so learn Christ!

—Ephesians 4:19–20

This is saying that from all of the understanding and knowledge that you have gained, these "sensual" things continue to manifest in your life on a daily basis. I am not talking about when you make a mistake every now and then. You do these things on a daily basis—to the point that you have become "willfully blind." Your heart has been hardened, and you have become insensitive to the fact that you are living a reckless life before God.

5. You indulge in every impurity that comes your way.

You may have learned the vocabulary of Scripture, but you have not learned Christ. You have not spiritually comprehended the purpose and reason why He died. Therefore, you have become prey to the influences of the world and the enemy. Since you have not learned Christ, you indulge in every impurity that comes your way. This is the fifth, and final, step. Verses 21–24 say:

Assuming that you have really heard Him and been taught by Him, as [all] Truth is in Jesus [embodied and personified in Him], strip yourselves of your former nature [put off and discard your old unrenewed self] which characterized your previous manner of life and becomes corrupt through lusts and desires that spring from delusion; and be constantly renewed in the spirit of your mind [having a fresh mental and spiritual attitude], and put on the new nature (the regenerate self) created in God's image [Godlike] in true righteousness and holiness.

Do you see a negative pattern forming in your life? If so, you need a new heart. The Spirit of the Lord does not govern the old heart because it does not belong to Him. It is the heart of Satan. So anything that Satan puts forth for us to do, if we have the old heart, we cannot rebuke it. We cannot say, "I refuse to do that," because we are housing his heart.

We must realize this heart is destined for eternal judgment. It will never lead you to life, because it does not have life in it. It will never lead you to eternal truth, because this heart does not have the ability to house the Word of the Lord.

> *Transformation takes place when our minds are brought to the understanding that we need God.*

THE DECEPTION OF THE FLESH

Before I move on to the works of the flesh, I want to make sure that you understand the fullness of what flesh means. It refers either to the physical body or the human nature (as opposed to the nature of God) with its "frailties...and passions." The flesh is you—in the natural—inside and out. The "internal" flesh is part of your old heart and your unrenewed mind, which causes the "external" flesh to disobey God.

> But I say, walk and live [habitually] in the [Holy] Spirit [responsive to and controlled and guided by the Spirit]; then you will certainly not gratify the cravings and desires of the flesh (of human nature without God). For the desires of the flesh are opposed to the [Holy] Spirit, and the [desires of the] Spirit are opposed to the flesh (godless human nature); for these are antagonistic to each other [continually withstanding and in conflict with each other], so that you are not free but are prevented from doing what you desire to do. But if you are guided (led) by the [Holy] Spirit, you are not subject to the Law.
>
> —GALATIANS 5:16–18

Verses 19–21 spell out the works of the flesh—read closely:

> Now the doings (practices) of the flesh are clear (obvious): they are immorality, impurity, indecency, idolatry, sorcery, enmity, strife, jealousy, anger (ill temper),

selfishness, divisions (dissensions), party spirit (factions, sects with peculiar opinions, heresies), envy, drunkenness, carousing, and the like. I warn you beforehand, just as I did previously, that those who do such things shall not inherit the kingdom of God.

These are just some of the characteristics of the heart that are being made manifest. Jeremiah 17:9 said that the

> *If people are veiled, they cannot see God. If their hearts are snared, they will surely die.*

heart is desperately wicked; who can know it? This must mean that we can only name some of the traits. Attached to these things, and behind them, are other things that have been "lodged" in the "old heart," things that have not yet come to light.

THE DECEPTION OF "CONTROL"

Have you ever been in a situation where you said to yourself, "I will never do this" or "I will never do that"? I cannot tell you how many times I said that I would never do something, and then ended up doing just that. This is because the old heart is on a timetable, to the degree that when it is allowed to remain within you, it becomes stronger by being fed the worldly knowledge from the brain. We "house" this old heart until every evil work from the bottom of the pit comes to the surface.

Think about it. How can a man walk into a school and start stabbing small children? Where does it come from? How can a person get a shotgun, walk into a McDonald's, and just start firing away and killing people? What do you think gets inside of a terrorist, causing him to ram a plane into the Twin Towers in New York City? These people did not simply plan to do these things. The depths of that evil heart were manifesting.

It starts small, with the things that you "think" you can control—which becomes the next deception of Satan. He allows you to think that you are in control of this "old heart." He allows you to think, *I have it under control. I only drank one drink.* Or, *I only smoked one cigarette.* He knows that if you keep going—keep letting that heart go unchallenged, unchanged, and unconverted—everything in that old heart (that he has birthed into the world) will be made manifest in your life.

Who can know this heart? Who would want this heart to remain in them, not knowing the full ability of evil that sits inside of them?

We have become walking time bombs. We have become accidents waiting to happen. We have become "accessible" to anything that Satan desires to do in the earth—a prey for his next assignment. How can you tell him no, when he is the ruler of that heart? It saddens me to think that the enemy's ways seem to be more "attainable" than the gospel—only because we have failed to ask God for a "new heart."

My *Heart Matters*

A Heart

CHAPTER 4

After God

This heart lives and thrives in an
atmosphere of worship.

$\mathcal{W}$E ALL HAVE A NATURAL HEART, BUT NOT MANY HAVE NEW HEARTS THAT THEY HAVE RECEIVED FROM GOD. In the natural realm, when a surgeon says that a heart transplant is necessary, it is a matter of life and death. This is the same in the spiritual realm. God has already said that the heart "is exceedingly perverse and corrupt and severely, mortally sick! Who can know it [perceive, understand, be acquainted with his own heart and mind]?" (Jer. 17:9). We desperately need a spiritual heart transplant!

God has already provided a donor for all who desire to undergo this vital procedure. The heart that rested inside of Jesus is available for transplant into your life. It is a heart of power. Jesus' heart came with an eternal assignment—and when we receive His heart, we receive our part of that mission.

A DIVINE CHARGE

When you receive a new heart, you can expect a battle. Your flesh, and the outside world, will not give up control without a fight. When God spoke to the Israelites, who because of the continual disobedience flowing out of their old hearts and their unrenewed minds that had

The new heart brings new warfare because the enemy wants to keep you bound and ineffective.

been taken captive and scattered out of the Promised Land, He gave them a divine charge:

> Therefore say, Thus says the Lord God: I will gather you from the peoples and assemble you out of the countries where you have been scattered, and I will give back to you the land of Israel. And when they return there, they shall take away from it all traces of its detestable things and all its abominations (sex impurities and heathen

religious practices). And I will give them one heart [a new heart] and I will put a new spirit within them; and I will take the stony [unnaturally hardened] heart out of their flesh, and will give them a heart of flesh [sensitive and responsive to the touch of their God].

—Ezekiel 11:17–19

God promised to gather His people and to give them back their land. But it wouldn't be without a fight! Along with their new heart would come the courage to take possession of their land and clean out all the impurities.

When Jesus talked with His own followers about living the "Christ life" with their new hearts, He said:

If the world hates you, know that it hated Me before it hated you. If you belonged to the world, the world would treat you with affection and would love you as its own. But because you are not of the world [no longer one with it], but I have chosen (selected) you out of the world, the world hates (detests) you. Remember that I told you, A servant is not greater than his master [is not superior to him].

—John 15:18–20

The good news is that Jesus overcame the world (John 16:33). He died to give us a healthy, new heart, and when that heart is transplanted inside of us, we have part of Jesus—the One who died and rose again—in our innermost being!

Every memory Jesus has of the Father, from before the foundation of the world, is inside of you. His experiences of walking with power and authority on earth and casting Satan down are stored in your new heart. Memories of when He rose from the dead and then ascended to sit on the right hand of the Father flow through your veins. Everything that God is—*since the dawn of eternity*—lives inside of you. If you have a new heart, you have supernatural power! The question is, *If we have truly received this new heart, how can we fail?*

If we trust and obey our new heart, Jesus will help us to get rid of all the "detestable things" and "abominations." Philippians 1:6 says:

> And I am convinced and sure of this very thing, that He Who began a good work in you will continue until the day of Jesus Christ [right up to the time of His return],

developing [that good work] and perfecting and bringing it to full completion in you.

In other words, Jesus will work inside of you until you do consistently what is pleasing to God (Phil. 2:13). If

> The new heart sets us free, dresses us for battle, and puts us right back into active duty.

you obey the Lord, your new heart will lead you through this life and into eternity. It is actually your deposit of eternity, because Christ has already passed through death and ascended to heaven.

He has made everything beautiful in its time. He also has planted eternity in men's hearts and minds [a

divinely implanted sense of a purpose working through the ages which nothing under the sun but God alone can satisfy], yet so that men cannot find out what God has done from the beginning to the end.

—ECCLESIASTES 3:11

God has an appointed time and a purpose for you on the earth. The only way you will fulfill that purpose and assignment is to trust and obey Him.

Therefore also now, says the Lord, turn and keep on coming to Me with all your heart, with fasting, with weeping, and with mourning [until every hindrance is removed and the broken fellowship is restored]. Rend your hearts and not your garments and return to the Lord, your God, for He is gracious and merciful, slow to anger, and abounding in loving-kindness; and He revokes His sentence of evil [when His conditions are met].

—JOEL 2:12–13

THE NEW HEART

The new heart is an amazing mystery, and we must walk in the Spirit to understand its depths. We hold the feelings and purposes of God within us! That is awesome.

> For who has known or understood the mind (the counsels and purposes) of the Lord so as to guide and instruct Him and give Him knowledge? But we have the mind of Christ (the Messiah) and do hold the thoughts (feelings and purposes) of His heart.
>
> —1 Corinthians 2:16

God tells us that He has a pattern for us to follow that will keep our new hearts alive. It is an atmosphere where our new hearts will thrive. It restores everything to a state of balance and harmony with God. It is the atmosphere of worship. In Joel 2:12, the Lord tells us to "turn and keep on coming to Me with all your heart, with fasting, with weeping, and with mourning [until every hindrance is removed and the broken fellowship is restored]."

God desires that we dedicate ourselves fully to Him, trusting in and obeying His instructions. As we do this, our new hearts are strengthened, and an atmosphere of righteousness, worship, and purification is created that reminds your heart of its heavenly home.

Your new heart comes from a purified place, so in order for it to be strong enough to stay in a willing position, you have to keep it in this type of atmosphere.

When a baby is delivered out of its mother's womb, the nurses wrap the baby up and hand it to the mother, who holds her baby close to her heart. This makes the newborn feel warm and protected, just like when that baby lived in the womb.

If you take a fish out of the ocean, it can survive as long as you put it back in water within a short period of time. You cannot take a fish out of the ocean, its place of origin where it survives and thrives, bring it home, and lay it on your living room table. It will never live like that. If you take it from water, where it is accustomed to living, you have to put it back into water in order for it to stay alive.

A fish will fight when you take it out of the water, and it is the same with the new heart. It "hungers and thirsts" after righteousness—it will suffocate if you take it out of God's presence. If you have a new heart, you should get to the point that you cannot get enough of God, church, or

God's people—because this heart lives and thrives in the atmosphere of worship.

Your new heart desires the things of God above the things of this world. You will find yourself saying, "I

Your new heart has the undeniable ability to walk in the statutes of God.

have to wash dishes, but I feel like glorifying God!" No longer will you have the thought ringing in your heart, *Oh no, I have to pray,* or *I have to go to church,* or *I have to worship.* Instead, as you prepare to go about your daily duties, getting ready for work, you will think, *I have to go to work, but I want to stay here in His presence!*

Your new heart will no longer sit in your pew at church and have to be forced to worship! No longer will you watch the clock as you hurriedly take three minutes to pray as your day begins. No longer will you have to deal with feelings of dislike or hatred toward your fellow man. Your new heart will compel you to love others.

This heart is bursting with the characteristics of Christ and longs for opportunities to express Christ through your actions. Because it "hungers and thirsts" for God, you must nourish it and feed it through your "Christ-life" living.

The new heart comes from glory—from God Himself, from heaven—where the heavenly host worships and praises Him continually. His glory, purification, righteousness, and awesome presence surrounded your heart like a warm blanket before He gave it to you. This heart cannot rest in the midst of junk. You have to put it in the same atmosphere out of which it was birthed.

My son, attend to my words; consent and submit to my sayings. Let them not depart from your sight; keep them in the center of your heart. For they are life to those who find them, healing and health to all their flesh. Keep and guard your heart with all vigilance and above all that you guard, for out of it flow the springs of life.

—Proverbs 4:20–23

My *Heart Matters*

Avoiding

CHAPTER 5

Heart Rejection

The Spirit of the Lord will never stay where He is not wanted.

$\mathcal{A}$ NEW HEART COMES WITH MANY GODLY ATTRIBUTES, INCLUDING A STRONG CONVICTION OF WHAT IT BELIEVES. God already "believes, accepts, and receives" Himself. He has every confidence that His Word is true. He knows it will accomplish His divine purpose. (See Isaiah 55:11.) We fall into error when we think of ourselves "more highly" than we should and then fail to trust and obey God. Isaiah 55:7–9 says:

> Let the wicked forsake his way and the unrighteous man his thoughts; and let him return to the Lord, and He will have love, pity, and mercy for him, and to our God, for He will multiply to him His abundant pardon. For My thoughts are not your thoughts, neither are your ways My ways, says the Lord. For as the heavens are higher than the earth, so are My ways higher than your ways and My thoughts than your thoughts.

Many in the church do not have the mind of Christ, so they live in a perpetual state of sin, saying, "I do not feel convicted about this. I do not feel bad about that."

Their consciences have become darkened, and they habitually do things that displease God. They do not love God or fear Him unto obedience.

When you have the new heart—God's heart—and you do anything that is contrary to God's Word, it will automatically send a wave of conviction. And because you love and fear God and believe in His name, you will repent.

He who believes in Him [who clings to, trusts in, relies on Him] is not judged [he who trusts in Him never comes up for judgment; for him there is no rejection, no condemnation—he incurs no damnation]; but he who does not believe (cleave to, rely on, trust in Him) is judged already [he has already been convicted and has already received his sentence] because he has not believed in and trusted in the name of the only begotten Son of God. [He is condemned for refusing to let his trust rest in Christ's name.] The [basis of the] judgment (indictment, the test by which men are judged, the ground for the sentence) lies in this: the Light has come into the world, and people have loved the darkness rather than and more than the Light, for their works (deeds) were evil. For every wrongdoer hates (loathes, detests) the Light, and will not come out into the Light but shrinks from it, lest his works (his deeds, his activities, his conduct) be exposed and reproved.

—JOHN 3:18–20

There is a penalty for sin, one way or the other. If you habitually do things that are ungodly and sense no

> *If you do not love God or fear Him unto obedience, you do not have the new heart.*

conviction, but just say, "God understands," the old heart has deceived you. You are walking out a death sentence.

THE DANGER OF HABITUAL SIN

When you reject the Word and do not put it into your heart and mind, the old nature assumes control—and you shut down the power and the activity of your new heart. God will not stay in this temple. You will have forced the Holy Spirit to leave, and not because you have done "one little thing" wrong. He will have left because you have refused to store the Word of God in your mind, enabling it to progress through all four stages of deliverance. You have refused to meditate on the Word. Therefore, your "emotional memories" and the stubbornness of your old mind can draw your heart to do something that offends God.

Anyone can make a mistake. Falling into temptation and sin does not mean that you are not saved. But when ungodly behavior becomes habitual to the point that you no longer sense the heart's conviction, the new heart has been repelled. Because you have ignored the new heart's correction—deliberately annihilating its message, which says that you no longer desire God—you have rejected your new heart. To consistently refuse the new heart's direction, you are sending a signal back saying, "I do not want you here." And the Spirit of the Lord will never stay where He is not wanted.

> *When you receive the new heart, its power breaks the shackles of things that possessed you as a sinner.*

THE TIME FOR CHANGE HAS COME

God is saying, loud and clear, that if we intend to live throughout eternity—if we intend to live for Him in this world—we need to change. If we don't, we will have massive heart failure and die a spiritual death. This is definitely a matter of the heart. Proverbs 4:23 says, "Keep and guard your heart with all vigilance and above all that you guard, for out of it flow the springs of life."

We must be vigilant, constantly examining our own hearts. Otherwise, we will continue to be the "great pretenders." One day the Lord may say to us, "Begone from Me…I never knew you" (Matt. 25:41; 7:23).

The Word of the Lord speaks to us from Revelation 2:5:

> Remember then from what heights you have fallen. Repent (change the inner man to meet God's will) and do the works you did previously [when first you knew the Lord].

As I close this chapter, heed this warning to care for your new heart diligently. Follow this advice from 2 Corinthians 13:5–11:

> Examine and test and evaluate your own selves to see whether you are holding to your faith and showing the proper fruits of it. Test and prove yourselves [not Christ]. Do you not yourselves realize and know [thoroughly by an ever-increasing experience] that Jesus Christ is in you—unless you are [counterfeits] disapproved on trial and rejected? But I hope you will recognize and know that we are not disapproved on trial and rejected. But

I pray to God that you may do nothing wrong, not in order that we [our teaching] may appear to be approved, but that you may continue doing right....

For we can do nothing against the Truth [not serve any party or personal interest], but only for the Truth [which is the Gospel]....And this we also pray for: your all-round strengthening and perfecting of soul. So I write these things while I am absent from you, that when I come to you, I may not have to deal sharply in my use of the authority which the Lord has given me [to be employed, however] for building [you] up and not for tearing [you] down.

Finally, brethren, farewell (rejoice)! Be strengthened (perfected, completed, made what you ought to be); be encouraged and consoled and comforted; be of the same [agreeable] mind one with another; live in peace, and [then] the God of love [Who is the Source of affection, goodwill, love, and benevolence toward men] and the Author and Promoter of peace will be with you.

God will be with us if we trust and obey our new heart. Above anything else, we must know that we have it.

My *Heart Matters*

Strengthening

CHAPTER 6

Your
New Heart

The more you seek God, the deeper
His counsel will become.

$\mathcal{E}$XPERIENCING THE FULLNESS OF GOD'S LOVE AND PRESENCE IN YOUR LIFE WILL BEGIN TO HAPPEN WHEN YOU HAVE YOUR NEW HEART. But unless you learn to use the keys of God's Word to unshackle your mind from the enemy's bondage, you will not be able to maintain His intimate presence in your life. Remember what Jesus said in Matthew 16:19:

I will give you the keys of the kingdom of heaven; and whatever you bind (declare to be improper and unlawful) on earth must be what is already bound in heaven; and whatever you loose (declare lawful) on earth must be what is already loosed in heaven.

We are to "bind" what God has already bound in His Word and to "loose" what He has already loosed. If you have received the new heart, both your heart and mind should be totally submitted to God's Word and ways. This is how you will begin to experience and walk in the "counsel" of God.

As you seek God in prayer, the Holy Spirit will begin to lead you into the counsel of God's Word. When you hear the voice of God in prayer, He will speak to you either through His Word (using His Word) or by speaking in harmony with what He has already revealed. The

> Once you have repented from habitual sin, you can then receive the "deep inner" meaning of His heavenly counsel.

more you seek God, the deeper His counsel will become and the more "secrets" He will reveal. You will gain more and more understanding. James 1:5 says:

If any of you is deficient in wisdom, let him ask of the giving God [Who gives] to everyone liberally and

ungrudgingly, without reproaching or faultfinding, and
it will be given him.

PRINCIPLES OF PRAYER AND INTERCESSION

Before you can begin to pray effectively, you need to
understand exactly what prayer is, so let us begin with
praise and petition. Yes, I started with praise, and, yes,
it works together with petition! You enter God's presence through your praises, because thanking God proves
your faith in Him to perform His Word. After all, if
you do not believe that God answers prayer, you might as
well not even ask—because He does not answer "double-
minded" requests. Philippians 4:6–7 says:

> Do not fret or have any anxiety about anything, but
> in every circumstance and in everything, by prayer and
> petition (definite requests), with thanksgiving, continue
> to make your wants known to God. And God's peace
> [shall be yours, that tranquil state of a soul assured
> of its salvation through Christ, and so fearing noth-
> ing from God and being content with its earthly lot
> of whatever sort that is, that peace] which transcends

all understanding shall garrison and mount guard over your hearts and minds in Christ Jesus.

There is also an intensified prayer of consecration where you press into God with a need to know or to do God's will. (See Matthew 26:39.) Another type of prayer is the prayer of faith, or an urgent request for God to intervene in a situation that usually requires an immediate answer. (See James 5:15.) The prayer of agreement is joining your faith with two or three others before God. (See Matthew 18:19–20.) Finally, intercession is when you pray and believe for someone else. (See Isaiah 59:16.)

There are also levels (or increasing intensities) of prayer:

> Keep on *asking* and it will be given you; keep on *seeking* and you will find; keep on *knocking* [reverently] and [the door] will be opened to you. For everyone who keeps on asking receives; and he who keeps on seeking finds; and to him who keeps on knocking, [the door] will be opened.
>
> —Matthew 7:7–8, emphasis added

Simply put, to ask is to petition God for your needs or to intercede for the needs of others. To seek means to ask God for deeper wisdom and, at the same time, to search the Word for deeper insight. Seeking can also mean that you study other resources or look more deeply

Sometimes we have to dig deeper, wait longer, and press in harder to get full revelation.

into the things around you. It can also mean that you receive godly counsel in order to get a full understanding of what God is saying.

Knocking is pressing in further through persistent prayer, fasting, and obedience to God's revealed and written Word. When you fast, you willingly give up food and anything else that stands in God's way in order to hear God, obey Him, and accomplish His purpose.

Fasting from food is extremely powerful because your new heart is bypassing your mind (which is bent on survival) and going directly to your body, which tells the brain, "Man shall not live and be upheld and sustained by bread alone, but by every word that comes forth from the mouth of God" (Matt. 4:4). To coin a phrase, fasting is "putting your body where your heart is" to squeeze out any form of mind control.

This is also why it is good to meditate even more deeply on the Word during a fast. It escalates the two-pronged counterattack to an all-out, three-pronged assault against the enemy. In other words, denying yourself food can help you to see that other "earthly" things are not that important—which opens the door to obedience in every area of your life. Ecclesiastes 4:12 says, "A threefold cord is not quickly broken."

When you overcome in a fast, the devil has to flee; there is a clear path—within you and outside of you— for God's will and purpose to be done. Let me say this a different way: when you overcome by denying yourself food, time, money, convenience, and whatever you value most, the devil will not be able to tempt you because you have already rejected everything that he can throw in your direction. And he cannot stay in the light; he has to run from it, because his evil deeds are immediately seen and exposed for what they truly are.

GETTING TO THE HEART OF PRAYER

Obviously, prayer is not what it needs to be in the body of Christ because we are operating from wicked, deceived hearts (Jer. 17:9). Prayer will be restored as we obey our new hearts and renew our old, stubborn minds. Today, in this season and final hour of the church, prayer will be the final test of any genuine believer or work for God:

Dwell in Me, and I will dwell in you. [Live in Me, and I will live in you.] Just as no branch can bear fruit of itself without abiding in (being vitally united to) the vine, neither can you bear fruit unless you abide in Me. I am the Vine; you are the branches. Whoever lives in Me and I in him bears much (abundant) fruit. However, apart from Me [cut off from vital union with Me] you can do nothing. If a person does not dwell in Me, he is thrown out like a [broken-off] branch, and withers; such branches are gathered up and thrown into the fire, and they are burned. If you live in Me [abide vitally united to Me] and My words remain in you and continue to live in your hearts, ask whatever you will, and it shall be done for you.

—JOHN 15:4–7

Prayer is our vital connection to God through the vehicle of our new hearts. If we do not pray, we will not have the life of Christ within us. We will be unproductive and, even worse, could be told on that Day, "I never knew you."

You must decide whether to hear and embrace this word of prophecy—and inherit eternal life—or to continue walking in your own thoughts and ways, and reap destruction. The choice is yours.

I pray and trust that you will choose to obey God and reap eternal life.

To get you started, the following are a few steps to develop your daily devotions, as well as a few Scripture keys on the heart and mind.

According to medicine, the heart transplant is immediate, but the mind transformation is progressive.

THE PRACTICE OF PRAYER*

I. Start each day loving God and people. This means your relationship with God is good

---

*I adapted this daily "prayer practice" from a powerful, in-depth teaching called "The Power of Positive Prayer Points," in Matthew Ashimolowo's special edition of the King James Bible. page 17. For more information regarding this resource, contact Matthew Ashimolowo Media Ministries, London, England, or go to his Web site at www.kicc.org.uk.

and that, as far as you are able, your relationships with family members, friends, co-workers, and others are in line with the Word.

2. Start each day communing with God through Bible study and prayer.

3. Thank God, praise Him for answering your prayers, and worship Him for who He is.

4. Repent, asking God to forgive you and to cleanse your heart from every sin, known and unknown.

5. Thank God for your spiritual armor, as listed in Ephesians 6:10–18.

6. Surrender yourself to the Holy Spirit so He can pray through you according to Romans 8:26–27.

7. Be ready to obey the Holy Spirit's leading, to petition (for your needs) or intercede (for

others); declare God's Word; lie still, or do whatever God leads you to do.

8. Ask God to build a hedge of protection around your life, family, and all others who are praying with you against the enemy's devices.

9. Ask God to rebuke Satan and all his servants.

10. Take authority over the enemy's work and his attempts to attack your new heart (spirit), your mind (emotions, logic, and decision making), and body.

11. Repeat these steps until you know that you have broken through in the Spirit realm and that God is leading you in prayer and intercession.

My *Heart Matters*

Prayer Keys
Heart

CHAPTER 7

for Your

and Mind

Love the Lord your God with all your mind and heart.

*H*ERE ARE A FEW SCRIPTURES TO GET YOU STARTED AS YOU SEEK GOD IN PRAYER DAILY, LEARNING TO EMBRACE YOUR NEW HEART. Put yourself in these scriptures as you meditate on the Word. For example, "I shall love the Lord my God with all my mind and heart."

> Create in me a clean heart, O God, and renew a right, persevering, and steadfast spirit within me....Let the words of my mouth and the meditation of my heart be acceptable in Your sight, O Lord, my [firm, impenetrable] Rock and my Redeemer.
>
> —PSALM 51:10; 19:14

> A new heart will I give you and a new spirit will I put within you, and I will take away the stony heart out of your flesh and give you a heart of flesh.
>
> —EZEKIEL 36:26

> Search me [thoroughly], O God, and know my heart! Try me and know my thoughts! And see if there is any

wicked or hurtful way in me, and lead me in the way everlasting.

—Psalm 139:23–24

Teach me Your way, O Lord, that I may walk and live in Your truth; direct and unite my heart [solely, reverently] to fear and honor Your name.

—Psalm 86:11

I delight to do Your will, O my God; yes, Your law is within my heart.

—Psalm 40:8

As for what was sown on good soil, this is he who hears the Word and grasps and comprehends it; he indeed bears fruit and yields in one case a hundred times as much as was sown, in another sixty times as much, and in another thirty.

—Matthew 13:23

And you shall love the Lord your God with all your [mind and] heart and with your entire being and with all your might.

—Deuteronomy 6:5

A FEW PRAYER KEYS FOR THE MIND

As I was studying, I found that the word *heart* is used at least seven times more in the Bible than the word *mind*. Many of these uses of the word *heart* refer to both heart

> *Your new heart comes from the Spirit realm, so you have to keep it in the atmosphere of the Spirit in order for it to exist.*

and mind, but I believe this is because the heart comes first—in the natural and spiritual realms. Begin to meditate on these scriptures:

> For who has known or understood the mind (the counsels and purposes) of the Lord so as to guide and instruct Him and give Him knowledge? But we have the mind of

Christ (the Messiah) and do hold the thoughts (feelings and purposes) of His heart.

—1 Corinthians 2:16

Do not be conformed to this world (this age), [fashioned after and adapted to its external, superficial customs], but be transformed (changed) by the [entire] renewal of your mind [by its new ideals and its new attitude], so that you may prove [for yourselves] what is the good and acceptable and perfect will of God, even the thing which is good and acceptable and perfect [in His sight for you].

—Romans 12:2

And be constantly renewed in the spirit of your mind [having a fresh mental and spiritual attitude], and put on the new nature (the regenerate self) created in God's image, [Godlike] in true righteousness and holiness.

—Ephesians 4:23–24

You will guard him and keep him in perfect and constant peace whose mind [both its inclination and its character] is stayed on You, because he commits himself to You, leans on You, and hopes confidently in You.

—ISAIAH 26:3

I will imprint My laws upon their minds, even upon their innermost thoughts and understanding, and engrave them upon their hearts; and I will be their God, and they shall be My people.

—HEBREWS 8:10

For God did not give us a spirit of timidity (of cowardice, of craven and cringing and fawning fear), but [He has given us a spirit] of power and of love and of calm and well-balanced mind and discipline and self-control.

—2 TIMOTHY 1:7

So brace up your minds; be sober (circumspect, morally alert); set your hope wholly and unchangeably on the grace (divine favor) that is coming to you when Jesus Christ (the Messiah) is revealed.

—1 PETER 1:13

Again, these verses will get you started. As you continue to seek, study, and meditate upon God's Word, He will finish the work that He has started in you.

The only thing that gives you control over the enemy is the synergy of the new heart and a renewed mind that is fully submitted to God and His will.

YOUR HEART MATTERS

Yes, the new heart message is a mandate for me to preach, because so many believers have been deceived (as I was) about their own hearts. So many think they are saved, but they still do not know Christ. Many leaders and preachers have not yet been born again, or they are not telling the whole truth and causing others to stumble.

Yes, knowing Christ has become "unattainable," but God can still deliver us.

God turned me around, so I know that He will do the same for you. Like me, you need to ask God to give you a new heart.

> Therefore also now, says the Lord, turn and keep on coming to Me with all your heart, with fasting, with weeping, and with mourning [until every hindrance is removed and the broken fellowship is restored]. Rend your hearts and not your garments and return to the Lord, your God, for He is gracious and merciful, slow to anger, and abounding in loving-kindness; and He revokes His sentence of evil [when His conditions are met].
>
> —Joel 2:12–13

Nothing is more important than the heart matters we have discussed in this little book. If you desire an intimate relationship with God above all else, ask God now for your new heart—because your heart matters.

My *Heart Matters*

New York Times best-selling author Juanita Bynum shares her heart!

What's Love got to do with it?
Just about Everything!

God must have big plans for you. He is still changing, refining, molding, and making you into His image every day because He loves you. Here are three more books by Juanita Bynum to help you along the way.

Discover the key to receiving your spiritual inheritance.

Prophetess Bynum explains how to receive all the blessings that God has for you when you live a life of obedience to Him and to those in spiritual authority over you.

ISBN 10: 1-59979-000-9
ISBN 13: 978-1-59979-000-8 / $14.99

The process of prayer never ends.

"Come with me…this journey is going to change your life for eternity…I believe this is a book that will be a lifelong manual for anyone with a passion to pray."

—Juanita Bynum

ISBN 10: 1-59185-803-8
ISBN 13: 978-1-159185-803-4 / $19.99

Is your heart sick?

Dig a little deeper and explore the heart/mind connection. See why this key to intimacy with God is so vital to a healthy, satisfying, and effective life.

ISBN 10: 0-88419-832-4
ISBN 13: 978-0-88419-832-1 / $13.99

Charisma HOUSE
A STRANG COMPANY
6658A

Visit your local bookstore.